Book Description

The fifties were a time of rebuild ̣... coming together following the horror and destruction of the Second World War that left Europe divided between the capitalist West and communist East. It was a time when TVs started to appear in most households, and a little thing called rock and roll began to creep into the mainstream music charts. Most of all, it was a time when the world showed itself to be so amazingly resourceful.

In a decade that gave us Elvis Presley and the Baby Boom, we can begin to see a theme growing already for what these years would have in store. People were learning to enjoy themselves again, but they never lost their determination and drive.

Hollywood was just coming into its Golden Age, and the movies that were being produced were so far ahead of their time that it was mind-boggling. Actors such as James Dean, Charlton Heston, and Marilyn Monroe all blossomed in the fifties. Films with the stature of *Ben Hur*, *Peter Pan*, and *Rebel Without a Cause* seemed to be coming out each month, as every genre imaginable was being explored.

In this book, we will take a leisurely stroll through one of the most astonishing decades of all time. You may cry, you might laugh, and on more than one occasion, you will look up from the book and wonder just how amazing this generation was...

A Trip Down Memory Lane

1950s Edition

Paragon Publishing

from various sources. Please consult a licensed professional before attempting any techniques outlined in this book.

By reading this document, the reader agrees that under no circumstances is the author responsible for any losses, direct or indirect, that are incurred as a result of the use of the information contained within this document, including, but not limited to, errors, omissions, or inaccuracies.

Table of Contents

Introduction

1950: South Africa Splits as the World Tries to Come Together

1951: Rock and Roll Is Born

1952: America Fears Communism and Polio Spreads

1953: Britain Is Shakin' But Not Stirred

1954: The King Is Born

1955: The Year of James Dean

1956: Revolution and Tea-Drinking Chimps

1957: Babies Boom

1958: Microchips and M1

1959: NASA Joins the Space Race

References

Introduction

Following the devastation of the Second World War, the whole world struggled to rebuild. Britain had been brought to its knees as the German bombs fell, and in the final five years of the forties, they survived on rationing and an indomitable spirit. The whole of Europe was in ruins, and America, Asia, and Africa all felt the effects of the worst war in history.

By the time the fifties rolled around, people were still dusting themselves off. Money was tight, with whatever remained being used by the world's governments to rebuild the cities that had fallen to the ground. Politicians were all suddenly susceptible to severe criticism, as the public demanded explanations for what had befallen them and the plans they had to bring the planet out of the mire.

Humankind has an astonishing spirit, and it is only when they have their backs to the wall that it truly comes out. Amazingly, when the world is at its darkest, that is when people seem to be at their most creative. Resourcefulness becomes essential, and this breeds new thinking. All of this spreads into music, entertainment, invention, and life itself.

The fifties typified a time when humankind showed some of its most extraordinary qualities. How else could a decade that had been born out of such devastation still be remembered as one of the most innovative and imaginative of all time? So many legends and geniuses prospered, and many more were born and molded to revel in the sixties.

One decade cannot exist without another, and when the one we are about to delve into gave us Elvis Presley, James Dean, Ralph Elison, Rosa Parks, and Martin Luther King Jr., to name but a few, we can begin to grasp just how important it was. It also gave birth to rock and roll, space flight, the microchip, and a PG Tips advert with chimps drinking tea.

Television boomed, and so did the birth of babies. Hair was slicked back, and a cheeseburger and a chocolate shake were all the teens needed to have a good time. Revolution was everywhere, and people were realizing that there was more to life than birth, work, and then death. There was music, movies, art, love, life, happiness, invention, sex, and a little thing called the jitterbug.

Trying to nail the fifties down to one single aspect is impossible, as it was a decade that created so much more. But when we look at it in terms of the mood it embodied, we can begin to see it as a time when the world began to realize its potential. It was a time when people's consciousness seemed to decide that they had suffered enough, and if they were going to push forward, then they would have to learn to enjoy themselves along the way.

So, sit back and let us begin our journey through the astounding decade that was the fifties...

1950: South Africa Splits as the World Tries to Come Together

The fifties bore witness to the Golden Age of Hollywood, among other things. It was a time when movie stars became more important than political figures or scientists, and the sight of one of these celebrities drew crowds that the US president himself would struggle to draw. In a moment in time when cinema was moving past slapstick and physical comedy to more dramatic, star-based movies, the stage was set for one James Dean to waltz into our lives. His good looks and considerable talent made him the world's hottest male lead for one glorious year, and his star would rise rapidly, only to burn out just as quickly.

By 1950, Dean was only turning 20, and his first appearance on TV came in the form of a Pepsi commercial. Although it was only a small role, his career would take off a few years later, and by '55, he would go on to star in several timeless classics. Dean would catch a trend in America that was really only rumbling in 1950. His image was that of a pop-culture legend, and he represents everything that Hollywood would come to stand for: Good looks, fast life, and glamor by the bucket load.

With the Cold War slowly heating up and the aftermath of the Second World War still being pieced together by

Europe and the rest of the world, America was booming in both economy and babies. It was fast becoming a sort of Dreamland, in which the people who didn't live there looked at it as something out of a futuristic movie. Clothes were sharper, dances were fresher, cars bigger, and food faster. For everyone else trying to rebuild after the devastation of the war, America was a place of wonder.

But through all of the glamor and technical advances lay an undercurrent of simmering anger. Race relations in America had long been a problem, and by the fifties, the minorities in the Land of the Brave had decided that they had had enough. As the African American population and other minorities that had been mistreated started to rise up, a wedge was slammed down between communities. America would have been aware of the rising tensions, but in South Africa, it had hit a whole new level of hatred.

Apartheid, which disgustingly translates simply as 'apartness,' had been introduced into South Africa in '48. Many had believed it wouldn't stick, as the severity of something as nasty as the segregation of all non-white civilians—which was a high majority—seemed so barbaric and unreal. The National Party, which had gained power two years before, was able to make such a move stick by referring to older policies of a time long gone, meaning that ratifying such laws proved shockingly easy. As people began to be separated and taught to hate one another, the wheels of a long, terrible time in South Africa's history were set in motion.

For those who thought that the end of the Second World War meant peace on Earth, they were quickly given a wake-up call. Conflicts still raged the world over, but since they weren't as severe as World War II, or at least not as close to home so far as the Western World was concerned, the public tried to push it to the back of their minds. They had been through a lot over the last few decades and quite rightly believed that they deserved a little peace of mind at last.

Asia had been rocked by the war too, and China made a move on Tibet in 1950 that led many people to believe that another World War was imminent. China had recently become a communist regime, a move that was enough to worry the United States, and they used the excuse that 'backward' Tibet needed China to bring them into the twentieth century. But the truth was that Tibet was lush with fertile land, and more importantly, held the Himalayan mountain range, which provided protection and military advantage over Nepal, India, and Bangladesh on the other side.

Another Asian country that had taken on communist ideals was North Korea, and they launched an attack on their Southern neighbors in early 1950. President Truman feared that if the weaker South Korea fell, Japan might be next, and the Americans needed the Japanese to continue the very lucrative trade they had built up. The fear of communism spreading to other parts of the globe would also have played a massive part, of course.

Swing music—and specifically swing dancing—had cooled in the mid-forties, but the early fifties saw a boom in teens boogie-woogieing their way across the dance floors once more. Dancing as a whole was still frowned upon in some parts of the world, and America and Britain were no different. But the kids didn't listen, and dances like the Bop, the Jitterbug, and the Lindy started to take off. The youth were beginning to feel some change in the air, and for the first time in a few decades, there was no worldwide war to take them away.

Music was becoming more rebellious by 1950. What was considered revolutionary in the style of songs in the fifties would make the kids of today laugh. Still, times were different, and the thought of children listening to anything harder than gospel or folk music was feared. But the winds were shifting, and almost like a sign of what was to come for the following few decades, Sam Philips launched a little record label in Tennessee called Sun Records. The artists that would come through the doors of Sun in the following years would read like a who's-who of musical legends.

The term "rock and roll" had yet to be coined, but the heavy, bluesy, angsty sound that had been played in African American neighborhoods and clubs for years was starting to be heard in the white parts of town. For most of the white folk who were not used to such music, they saw this style as 'evil' or "devil's music." Luckily, a young 15-year-old kid by the name of Elvis Presley was growing up in a predominantly African American part of the town of Tupelo Mississippi at the beginning of the decade, and the influence that this music would have on him would change the way people viewed music forever.

It speaks volumes for how stubborn the Western World was at the time that it took a white man to play African American music before it became socially acceptable to record and listen to it, and even then, it was still heavily oppressed by the general public. But if that is what it took to get rock and roll out there, then it was going to have to do. The charts at the time were still filled with artists such as Frank Sinatra, Bing Crosby, and Jo Stafford, and they would remain legends for eternity. Still, something else was happening, and only the most arrogant of people would try to resist it.

The World Cup in Brazil saw England take part for the first time in their history, having deemed the competition beneath them up until then. Even though they went in as one of the favorites, they were humiliated, losing both of their matches 1-0 to America and Spain. Brazil had spent a fortune setting up the competition and had even gone so far as to build the fabulous Maracana Stadium from scratch. The hosts went on to lose the final to second-time winners Uruguay in front of a staggering 205,000 people.

Amazingly, Brazil had thought themselves guaranteed winners, and the local newspapers had gone so far as to print the following morning's papers before kick-off. The front page showed the Brazilian team photo and the word "champions" above it. Some people reading it the following morning knew no different and celebrated their nation lifting football's most precious prize.

With TV coverage almost non-existent at the time, especially in South America, a small village in Minas Gerais, Brazil, gathered around a transistor radio to listen to the game unfold. Upon finding his father crying in his room after the final whistle, a 9-year-old Pele told his dad not to worry; he would win him a World Cup one day. He won three for him (Pele, 2006).

In Britain, Princess Elizabeth and Prince Philip gave birth to their only daughter, Princess Anne, in August. In a country that still idolized its royals, the nation rejoiced. Princess Anne would remain a favorite of the public to this day, and she even went on to compete in the Olympic Games in 1976, riding a horse that belonged to her mother. Her love for the Olympics would remain throughout her life, and she became a member of the International Olympic Committee some time later.

Cases of polio were rising, and by 1950, it seemed that nowhere on the globe was safe from the horrible disease. Kids everywhere were being forced to isolate, and thousands would be paralyzed as it spread with ease. Many more would die, and as it ripped through the towns and cities, parents cried out for a cure. It would take a while yet, and the public would have to live in the hope that a breakthrough could be made sooner rather than later.

The Golden Age of Hollywood was starting to take shape by 1950, and American sport was growing too. It would take another few years for the latter to become the phenomenon that it did from the sixties onward, though. Still, national interest was increasing due to more easily accessible radio coverage and commercial TVs. Unlike football (soccer) in Europe—and especially Britain—the people of America had to travel thousands of miles to catch a game in their chosen sport if it was an away fixture. This meant that keeping tabs on their favorite team could only be done by waiting for the following morning's papers.

All of that was changing, though, and technology and more demand for national sports meant that the public would soon have much easier access to watch the events they desired. Music was becoming something different too, and along with all of the new dances, that thing called rock and roll was starting to seep out of the underground clubs and bars. The Second World War was five years in the past, and the younger people were beginning to lift their heads and face forward once more.

Everything that was needed to raise the revolutionary generation of the sixties was starting to blossom in the fifties, and freedom of thought and expression were being found in the far reaches of a once buttoned-down society. We now know how vitally important the fifties were, but as it began, all the public knew was that something had changed. What it was, they couldn't have been sure of yet.

1951: Rock and Roll Is Born

A snap election in Britain, instigated by the Labour Party who wanted to tighten its grip on its parliamentary majority, backfired when the Winston Churchill-led Conservative Party won the vote and regained power. It was a bold move by Labour, who had won the general election only 18 months prior, and one that would prove devastating to their hopes in the long run. Churchill's return to power would set in motion a 13-year stay at the top for the Conservatives. How Labour underestimated the popularity of Churchill is anyone's guess. However, they did, and the most loved politician in British history proved that the public still saw him as the way forward, despite his age.

Fifties Britain was a lot different than it is today. Most of the ladies wore long dresses, and the men, suits. For the youth, the Teddy Boy look was growing, with a lot of this due to the ever-growing influence of American culture and the likes of James Dean being seen on cinema screens. Sweets, petrol, and sugar were still rationed, as Britain continued to pay off debts accumulated during the Second World War. Several bomb shelters stood unused under London (and still do today!), but the constant fear that had filled the hearts of the nation—and the rest of the world—was beginning to fade. Other worries in the form of polio, poverty, and social tensions had replaced it, though.

In an attempt to boost national pride and to promote the post-war economy, the Festival of Britain was held to great acclaim. The main events were on London's South Bank, an area that would later be home to great cultural venues such as the National Theatre and Tate Modern. Exports were on the rise at least, as the income needed to rebuild after the devastation of the war could not be accumulated through local trade alone. The docks of Liverpool, Southampton, London, Leith, Holyhead, and many others were extremely busy. They were a place where a lot of the employment came, but the conditions were terrible, and the pay was low. Yet that feeling of hope remained, never more proven than by the re-election of Winston Churchill, a man that the public believed understood their plight more than anyone else. His spirit reflected those of Britain and the rest of Europe, and that spirit was one of never giving up.

America, on the other hand, was starting to prosper again. Hollywood and the music scene seemed to paint the whole nation in vibrant colors. Diners of red and white and fairgrounds filled with cotton candy became the image of perfect Americana, and from the outside looking in, it represented freedom and opportunity. For the people who lived there, they carried an air of determination and drive.

Alan Freed, an American disc jockey, coined the term "rock and roll" in '51. He became a pioneer in promoting African American music on his radio show, which most of North America heard, believing that all people should listen to whatever music they wanted to. This belief drove him to play harder, more rock-based music throughout his show. For the parents who were still a bit too straight-laced, he was a menace. But for the younger people who wanted to listen to the stuff they had only heard leaking out of the clubs, he was a revolutionary.

The term "rock and roll" was only used by Freed in an attempt to cover the fact that he was playing rhythm and blues, which was considered by most white folk to represent African American music. It is a sad sign of where the world was at the time in that he had to go to these lengths to promote something that is so magical. But much like Elvis continuing to break down barriers in the following years, it needed to be done if he was to bring a brand of music that represents everything good about us as humans to the masses.

The charts in '51 were still dominated by the crooners of the decade before and violin-based numbers, but the times were changing, and if you didn't get with the rock and roll trend, then you weren't a "cool cat," and you could just go and "get bent." Leather jackets and short-sleeve shirts were all the rage among young men, and seeing someone with a pack of cigarettes tucked into their sleeve was not uncommon. There was a rebelliousness to the youth, but it was still only whispered over a chocolate malt and a cheeseburger.

On June 25, 1951, CBS broadcast for the first time in color, although this wonder was limited to North America, and even then, only for a select few. In 1948, only 1 million TVs—all black and white—had been purchased in America. By '51, it was up to 10 million. Color TVs were still in their infancy, but this amazing invention could still be seen in the electrical stores of every town, and for the families that could afford them, they became an instant hangout spot for all of the neighborhood kids. Shows such as *I Love Lucy* and *The Colgate Comedy Hour* were becoming popular. TV was starting to be aimed at a younger generation, as they were the ones more likely to buy the clothes and gadgets advertised during the many ad breaks.

Employment was growing in America, and the Depression and world wars of the previous decades were being left in the past. Traffic was also increasing due to the rapid growth in the economy, and in '51, the country completed the construction of the New Jersey Turnpike. The mammoth road helped loosen the cluttered traffic somewhat. Still, it would need to continue expanding throughout the years to cope as the population and car ownership continued to explode.

Many of the vehicles on the roads and highways were imported, and cars made by companies such as Volkswagen and Austin were most popular. The European car trade was one of the only things that was keeping Britain and the rest of Europe standing, and the income it created was so important. European cars were seen as more reliable, and the American public needed as many as they could get their hands on. It was a situation that worked out pretty well for both sides of the Atlantic, at least for a while.

With Britain in quite a dark place, they had to watch as America boomed. One piece of respite and national pride came when British boxer Randolph Turpin upset all the odds by beating heavy favorite Sugar Ray Robinson to become the middleweight champion of the world. He was the first British man to hold the title in 60 years, and the victory lifted the spirits of a nation.

Being such an underdog, Turpin had been forced to sign a contract that stipulated he must fight Sugar Ray a second time—within 90 days of the first fight—if he was to win somehow. The second fight would go the distance, but Turpin would only hold the title for 64 days.

The World Series saw a monumental first and last in the final. Legend of the game, Joe DiMaggio retired following the Yankees third straight championship, but a young Mickey Mantle began his career, so the game lost one hero and gained another. The Yankees, who had thrashed the Phillies in the final the year before, lifted the title once more as they beat crosstown rival the Giants 4-2. The hero of the sixth game was Hank Bauer, but it will always be remembered more fondly for DiMaggio's last appearance.

In England, two of football's biggest underachievers actually managed to lift silverware in '51, as Tottenham Hotspur and Newcastle United won the league title and the FA Cup, respectively. A season of shocks saw the mighty Everton relegated from the top division for only the second time in their history, which was seen as nothing short of a disaster for a club of their stature. The second-place finish for Manchester United proved that Matt Busby was building a force to be reckoned with, and his youthful side was first nicknamed the Busby Babes in the 50/51 season. Their time to shine would be devastatingly cut short in a few years.

While Hollywood was booming and America glittered, a more conservative Britain had other ideas regarding cinema and its effect on their youth. The British Board of Film Classification (BBFC) introduced an X rating for movies for the first time, meaning that no one under the age of 16 could view any film with such a tag attached. At a time when a movie theater was the only place for the public to watch blockbuster films, it was a real blow for the kids who wanted to see what all of the older kids on the estate were waxing lyrically over.

By the time '51 came to a close, the Western World was split, in so far as economy and infrastructure went. While America seemed to prosper by the day, Europe lagged behind. The export of cars and other products across Europe brought in quite a bit of revenue for the time being, and jobs would soon be on the rise as the social and economic infrastructure grew in strength. But the people of Britain and the rest of the continent had been through this sort of thing before, and they always came out the other side stronger than when they went in. Winston Churchill's return was like a phoenix rising from the ashes, and it inspired hope in the public.

Alan Freed had coined the term "rock and roll" earlier in the year, and that feeling of rebelliousness would soon spread across the globe. Unbeknownst to the older generation, it would be a blessing in disguise, as the youth would use it to fight against conformity and declare that the world's current situation was just not good enough. "Be grateful for what you have" was not something they would abide by anymore, especially since what they had was nothing.

Economic growth was coming, and there was an innocence to the fifties that was never more evident than at the birth of the decade. Moral standards were still amicable, and respect was something that the kids seemed to be born with. Regardless of the teenagers' and young adults' need to stand up for what they believed in, they would do so with honor and hard work. This was never more evident than in '51, when a bleak past was not looked back on with self-pity but instead used as inspiration to build a brighter future.

1952: America Fears Communism and Polio Spreads

The Red Scare—a sort of mass hysteria surrounding the threat of fierce war between the Soviets and the USA—intensified in the early fifties. The first time it had happened had been before World War I, but new fears arose following the end of the Second World War and the birth of the Cold War in the late 1940s. The term 'red' was often used to describe a communist, and things were taken up another level in March of '52 when the Supreme Court upheld a New York state law that prohibited communists from teaching in public schools. It was a time of great suspicion and betrayal among friends and neighbors, as the public lived by the rule of "trust no one."

The fear of nuclear war wasn't just affecting the United States and the Soviet Union. In October of '52, Great Britain detonated an atomic bomb at the Montebello Islands off the coast of Western Australia. The test was a way of not only knowing the power they could unleash if needed but also letting the other two superpowers know that they would not be pushed around. It was a challenging and confusing time, as the more powerful nations had to decide whether to invest in nuclear weapons or dismiss them. The only problem with the latter was that they left themselves wide open to being destroyed if war *did* break out.

Across the globe, scientists and doctors were being stretched to their limits as thousands more cases of polio were reported. The epidemic was striking fear into the hearts of children and parents alike, and images in the newspapers of kids isolated in tiny chambers or locked away in their bedrooms for safety only added to the feeling of helplessness. By '52, cases had spiked at over 55,000 in the States alone, and the disease was putting many children in wheelchairs and iron lungs. It was a horrific time, but as we know by now, the human spirit is strong, and it always finds a way to fight through.

In South Africa, the apartheid ruling was causing severe tensions. However, a man named Nelson Mandela had formed a group of revolutionaries who would fight tooth and nail to stop it. This would lead to him being imprisoned in July for a nine-month sentence of "hard labor," a move that only hardened his determination. His anti-apartheid stance was deemed communist by those in charge, which gave the court free rein to sentence him quickly. Mandela would be jailed many times for his beliefs, but he would not rest until he had achieved everything that he had set out to do.

The Diary of a Young Girl, also known worldwide as *The Diary of Anne Frank*, was first published in the US in '52. It had been published in many other countries before then, but the US version seemed to be the one that caused the words on the pages to become public knowledge. If anyone hadn't known the full severity of the horrors caused by Nazi Germany before then, they surely did now. Something about the perspective of a frightened—yet extremely courageous—girl in the Netherlands hiding from the Gestapo broke the hearts of all who read the book. It would go on to inspire a Pulitzer Prize-winning play, movies, and many TV series and is unanimously known as the most famous diary ever written.

The first Holiday Inn opened its doors in America when construction on a small motel was finished in August. It was situated on the main highway to Nashville, Tennessee, which was the home of its creator Kemmons Wilson. The style of the Holiday Inns represented everything that America was about at the time: fast, efficient, brash, and colorful. Many more would rapidly pop up over the following years. By 1993, they were the largest chain of motels in the world, and today, there are a reported 1,276 branches across the globe.

TV continued to boom, and the maiden airing of the morning news and talk *Today Show* occurred in '52. It was the first program of its kind the public had ever seen. Its blend of daily news interspersed with slap-stick comedy—and even a chimp named J. Fred Muggs—became a staple of American breakfast routines soon to be seen as important as Lucky Charms and coffee. Following the success of NBC's *Today Show*, many other television companies followed suit, and the US soon had ABC's *Good Morning America* and CBS's *The Early Show* airing alongside it. The rest of Europe wasn't so quick to accept this trend of lowbrow early morning news reporting, and Britain had to wait until 1983 until the dross of *Good Morning Britain* woke them up each morning.

In cinema, the technicolor extravaganza *The Greatest Show on Earth* was all the rage. The movie won two Academy Awards for Best Picture and Best Story and featured the beloved James Stewart as a mysterious clown who remains in character—and makeup—on and off the stage. It was another success for director/producer Cecil B. DeMille, whose golden touch had created the year's biggest blockbuster. He seemed to do this quite often, and his 70 films, both silent and sound, are widely regarded as one of the most remarkable bodies of work in cinematic history.

One movie that somehow slipped under the radar and only shows the quality of films being made at the time was *Singin' in the Rain*. The Gene Kelly-choreographed masterpiece was only the tenth-highest grossing film of '52, and its cult status would take time to grow. In hindsight, it is now seen as the greatest musical ever made and has gone on to inspire so many more in the genre. Kelly starred in the movie, too, alongside Donald O'Connor and Debbie Reynolds. Despite the relatively low return on such a classic, it *was* recognized during awards season, winning a few and being nominated for many more.

With television now taking off in Britain as well, the first-ever TV detector van was rolled out in February. The van, designed to decipher which homes had TVs, was brought in to catch anyone doing so without a television license. Britain and Ireland were—and still are, in some cases—a little different from the rest of the world when it came to owning a TV, and their governments claimed that enjoying channels such as BBC or RTE was not a privilege that should come for free. People who wanted to splash out their yearly wage on a television set then had to fork out an annual fee in taxes to watch it. The sight of the cream-colored van with its huge aerial prowling the streets of Britain and

Ireland would often cause the local kids to sprint home in fear, shouting at their family to switch the TV off. It was like some twisted evil twin of the Ice Cream Man.

A Britain that was already in a dark place opened and closed the year with even more tragedy. On February 6, 1952, King George VI died quietly in his bed. The Second World War had taken its toll on the royal leader, and his stress levels coupled with his heavy smoking—and the lung cancer it caused—would lead to his untimely death at the age of 56. His oldest daughter, Princess Elizabeth, had been taking on a lot of his royal duties in the preceding few years as his health deteriorated, and she was able to step in quite seamlessly after his death, despite her sadness. Her crowning would have to wait, though, as she was in Kenya at the time on a royal tour.

In December of '52, another event shook Britain, and London in particular, when the Great Smog of London caused havoc. The city's heavy reliance on burning coal and the growing population in such a small area coincided with a cold snap. This drop in temperature was aided by another shift in weather, and almost no breeze blew for nearly four days. The smog, mostly made up of pollutants, gathered in a heavy cloud above the city, and as it descended, it even managed to affect those who locked themselves away indoors.

Almost 100,000 people were taken ill over the four days, and as the wind shifted on the final day and the smog cleared somewhat, over 4,000 deaths were reported. This amount has been greatly challenged over the years, and many experts believe the total number of fatalities to be closer to 12,000. Whatever the case may be, Britain as a whole seemed to be getting kicked relentlessly while it was down.

One small bit of solace, at least so far as the public's national pride was concerned, came a couple of weeks later when the soon-to-be crowned Queen Elizabeth II gave her maiden Christmas Message. Her father had done it in previous years, but always on the radio, but this was the first time it would be televised. For the people of Britain to see the young queen's valiant, youthful face on TV screens as she told them to remain strong was an inspiring moment and one that helped them to look into the new year with a little hope.

In a year that saw the death of a royal and a spike in polio, it would have been easy for the people of the fifties to give up and accept the world as it was, but that was not the mentality of the hardest working generation in history. For those who lived in this time, it was just another thing that they needed to get through and come out stronger on the other side, and they would do just that. In fact, even in '52, the world was making lasting changes to the way the next generation would live. Along with the advances in television, music, and electrical appliances, came a much stronger infrastructure that didn't just favor the wealthy for once.

Housing estates were popping up all over, and although many of them were grim places to live, they were still communities that before then didn't even exist. And "community" will always be one of the best ways to describe the fifties. For the parents who had survived the devastation of the Second World War, they wanted nothing more than for their kids to live a hardworking, honest life. They had lived through the fear of falling bombs, and they brought their young ones up to appreciate all they had, even if it wasn't much.

This would change later in the decade and continue into the sixties when the youth demanded more than the bare minimum. But for now, the world was in the early stages of rebuilding, and to do that, they needed the whole community to stand together as one.

1953: Britain Is Shakin' But Not Stirred

It was nearly a year and a half after the death of King George VI that his eldest daughter, Elizabeth, was crowned Queen Elizabeth II at the tender age of 27. Her coronation took place on June 2, 1953. Part of the wait was down to the rule that any such festivities should not be celebrated so soon after the death of a royal, especially one as important as the King. For a nation that had already been through the wringer, the first-ever televised coronation at Westminster Abbey went a long way in lifting spirits. National pride was also boosted by the simultaneous news that the British Mount Everest expedition had succeeded in putting two mountaineers on the summit of the highest peak in the world: Sherpa Tenzing Norgay and New Zealander Edmund Hillary.

Another breakthrough in '53 that helped bring insurmountable joy and relief to Britain and the rest of the world was the creation of a polio vaccine. Although the research had been conducted for a while, many vaccines had been tried and failed throughout the years. When American medical researcher Dr. Jonas Salk announced that he had finally made the breakthrough on national radio, there was trepidation among the public. Their hearts had been broken before by such proclamations, and there was still a fear that the vaccine wouldn't work. For the thousands of kids already suffering from the disease, it was too little too late.

Another plus for humankind was the signing of the Korean Armistice Agreement, which effectively ended the Korean War. After three years of horrific fighting, North Korea, South Korea, the People's Republic of China, and America agreed to lay down their arms and call it a draw, so to speak. President Dwight D. Eisenhower, who had criticized Harry S. Truman's handling of the Korean War in the lead-up to the election the previous year, kept his promise of ending it after he came into power. The fact that Eisenhower achieved this by threatening nuclear war became secondary, and whether he actually ever would have resorted to such things remains unclear.

Even with the Korean War all but over, the Cold War was still a concern and would be for a while. Tensions between the Soviets and Americans had never been so bad, and unbeknownst to everyone on the planet, things would soon heat up even more. Their latest battle would not take place on land, though, or even in the Earth's atmosphere, but in space. All of that would come a few years later when the Space Race really took off.

In '53, America's biggest fear seemed to be the threat of communism. Being a 'red' was seen as the worst thing a person could be, and it would soon be a term used for anyone who questioned the direction the United States government was moving in. Looking back, it was an extremely clever tactic by the powers that be to use the fear of communists in America against their own people. Now, Americans had to accept any decision made by their leaders with complete and utter trust or be considered an enemy of the state. It was something—ironically like communism—that worked in theory, but it could never last.

As the "trust no one" attitude spread through America, J. Edgar Hoover and his team of FBI agents began rounding up known communists who they had been keeping an eye on for a while. Many men, women, and children were brought in for questioning, and the public's suspicions reached a fever pitch. Conspiracies were everywhere, and many scenes at the time took on a sort of Hollywood detective movie feel. But the allegations, sentences, and deaths that occurred during this time were all real.

The death of Joseph Stalin in March might have made the world think that communism would maybe perish with him, but the hundreds of thousands of mourners who crammed the streets of Moscow in the days following his passing quashed any such beliefs. The hysteria in the crowd was so severe that over 100 people died after being crushed as the Russian people tried everything they could to get one last look at the man that they adored and feared in equal measure. China, which had themselves embraced these communist ideals under Chairman Mao, announced a day of mourning to commemorate Stalin's death.

Sweets, petrol, and sugar, which had been rationed in Britain since the war, came back onto the market in February. The kids who had been saving their shillings for so long were finally allowed to indulge their sweet tooth after years of waiting, and the always popular toffee apples were the biggest sellers. Other delicious sweets of the day, including licorice strips and sticks of nougat, also flew off the counter, proving that Britain was finally starting to see some light at the end of the tunnel.

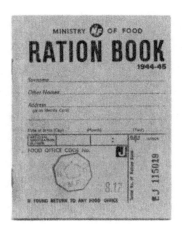

As the economy started to see its first upturn in fortune for years, the prosperity spread into the football league too, and Sir Matt Busby splashed out £29,999 on a young Tommy Taylor. The Yorkshireman was only 21 when he signed for United, and to relieve some of the pressure of being the most expensive player in the history of British football, Sir Matt asked for the fee to be one pound less than £30,000. The signing wouldn't work out as planned at first, as the reigning champions finished a disappointing eighth.

The closest league title up until that point played out in 52/53, and Arsenal pipped Preston North End on goal difference. Amazingly, this record would stand until 1989, when Arsenal again would claim the title, this time by one single goal scored in injury time on the final day. In the FA Cup, Sir Stanley Matthews finally got his hands on the trophy he had sought after his whole life at the sweet old age of 38, playing for Blackpool. The final would be forever known as the Matthews Final, even though the superb Stan Mortenson scored a hat-trick, thanks to Sir Stanley's magical display.

Stateside, the NFL saw the Detroit Lions defeat the Cleveland Browns for the second year in a row. It was the first year where the National and American conferences were referred to as Eastern and Western conferences. The naming made little difference, but the league was constantly expanding in both size and popularity, and American football was rapidly becoming the American public's most loved sport.

Basketball saw the second part of a three in a row title-winning streak for the Minneapolis Lakers. The franchise, which would move to Los Angeles in a few years' time, was soon to begin their legendary rivalry with the Boston Celtics that dominated basketball in the sixties. The final in '53 also saw the completion of another triple, but it wasn't a record that New York Knicks would be proud of, as it was their third straight loss in the final. The Knicks would have to wait until 1970 for their first-ever NBA championship win.

In music, "Crazy Man Crazy" by Bill Haley & His Comets became the first rock and roll song in history to break into the *Billboard 100 Chart*. This tiny ripple in the sea of the music world would soon become a tidal wave, and the undercurrent of rock and roll was starting to move in a little recording booth in Sun Studios, Memphis. Elvis Presley was only 18 when he met pioneer Sam Phillips, and the songs that The King would record at Sun would shape the way the world views music from that point onward. When added to Elvis's unique voice, his mix of rhythm and blues, country, rockabilly, bluegrass, and gospel all morphed into that raw new sound called rock and roll.

Cinema saw the release of the second big Disney full-length animation movie of the fifties, the first being the massively successful *Cinderella*. The second, the magical tale of Neverland and the kids who never grew up there, *Peter Pan*, drew unanimous admiration from critics and fans alike. It would finish an impressive 5th in the box office at the end of the year and was one of several movies released by Disney in an era that is generally thought to be their Golden Age.

James Bond made his first appearance in any form when the publication of *Casino Royale* in '53 catapulted the protagonist and author Ian Flemming into the public domain. It would be another decade until 007 would hit the silver screen, but his name had been put on the entertainment map, and one of the most famous and recognizable fictional characters in history was born.

Years before, Fleming, a Commander in the National Intelligence Division (NID), had actually led a group who formed an Allied spy operation in 1943 to monitor Spain during World War II, as fears that they were about to align with Franco began to spread. The operation, which was put in place to ensure that Britain could still communicate with Gibraltar if Spain did turn, never needed to be carried out in the end. Many of the experiences that Flemming would have in his military position would all help him to mold his James Bond creation. The name of the operation in'43? *Operation Goldeneye.*

The discovery of the fossilized remains of an "early human" in 1912 by amateur archeologist Charles Dawson had rocked the scientific world. Dawson's find, which only slightly resembled human remains, was severely questioned by parts of the scientific community, yet it continued to be called the "missing link between ape and man" for four decades. It wasn't until 1953 that Dawson (who had died in 1916) was proved to be a forger, and several of his hoaxes, including the aforementioned Piltdown Man, were finally debunked. It is considered one of the most famous hoaxes in the history of science, both because of the worldwide exposure it caused and the 40-year gap between its discovery and being proven as a fake.

The first significant sales of color TVs commercially picked up in '53, as families began to splash out on one of the most impressive inventions to date. Consumerism as a whole was growing, mainly in the western world, as employment started to become more readily available. The darkness of the Second World War was finally beginning to be left behind, and although the people would never forget, they knew that to heal, they had to keep pushing onward and upward.

It seemed that by '53, the world was finally getting on its feet again. The fear of nuclear war remained, and talk of war with the Soviets hung over America like a dark cloud. But TV and music were the things that were exploding, and there was a feel-good factor in the air. The end of rationing in Britain reflected this, as the public began to live the life that they rightly felt they deserved. Almost like Peter Pan himself, the kids were finally being given a chance to blossom, and they were going to fly as high as they could with it.

1954: The King Is Born

The year 1954 continued to bring better news, and the first large-scale use of the polio vaccine rolled out across America in February. It would have an immediate effect. At a time when 180 cases per 100,000 people were the norm, the fall to 20 in the same number in its first year of being administered was huge. It was another major scientific breakthrough in a series of many, especially in the medical profession, and through the years, millions of patients who would previously have been deemed a lost cause made recoveries and went on to live full lives.

The last cases of polio would not be completely eradicated for another few decades. Still, following the breakthrough made by Dr. Salk the previous year and the subsequent global use of the vaccine, the cases would drop drastically, bringing an end to the waking nightmare that had terrorized parents the world over. It was another bright moment for a decade that was really starting to find its feet.

This was also evident when the British Medical Council first announced that they were linking smoking to lung cancer. Amazingly, before then, smoking—although known to be unhealthy—had never been fully associated with cancer. Whether it was something that people just didn't want to hear at the time or something more sinister, the first admission of the detrimental effects of smoking cigarettes was another huge step in the world becoming more aware. People were starting to realize that there were things that they could do to prolong their lives, and living healthy was the way to do it.

In the world of music, an astonishingly rapid rise for one pop star had begun early in the year and reached heights that the soon-to-be King of Rock and Roll—or anyone for that matter—could have foreseen. Although young Elvis Presley had recorded a few songs in Sun Studios the previous year, it wasn't until his newly-formed backup band began messing around with a souped-up version of "That's All Right (Mama)" in-between takes that Sun owner Sam Phillips saw the future of music at that very moment.

Phillips asked guitarist Scotty Moore and bassist Bill Black to play the jam again, and he sat back in awe as Elvis began to find his range and lay down his lung-busting flawless vocals on the track. They followed that up with a dirty, bluesy version of "Blue Moon of

Kentucky," which was so heavy that Scotty Moore was heard saying that they would be run out of town for tearing up such a beloved classic. Instead, the double-sided single was played on WHBQ for the first time the following morning, and by the time the radio went off the air that evening, it had been played 14 more times. The King was born.

The biggest box office draws of '54 showcased a who's who of Hollywood legends. The highest-grossing film of the year was the timeless *White Christmas*, starring Bing Crosby. It would, of course, spawn Crosby's cover of the title track, which had originally been released in 1942, and with sales of over 50 million copies, remains the largest selling physical single of all time.

Other stars who graced the silver screen that year were Humphrey Bogart in *The Caine Mutiny*, which finished second at the box office and went on to be nominated for a whopping seven Academy Awards. Kirk Douglas starred in the big-budget *20,000 Leagues Under the*

Sea, as Disney Productions switched back to live-action following the huge success of the animated *Peter Pan* the previous year. There were also huge successes for Judy Garland in *A Star is Born* and James Stewart in the Alfred Hitchcock-directed *Rear Window.* Hollywood's Golden Age was in full swing.

Everything seemed to be getting bigger, cooler, and faster, and this was again proven with the release of the new Mercedes-Benz 300 SL Coupe. The sleek "super light (SL)" car was the first to showcase their futuristic "gullwing" doors that popped open at the sides and swung upward. It was a representation of how the world was moving past things like rationing and rebuilding after the war and moving on to extravagances such as fancy cars and color TVs.

In the space of a couple of months, the United States government proved that not much had changed in their views on immigration and their fear of non-Americans. In June of '54, Joseph Swing, the Director of US Immigration, put forth the initiative to remove all Mexican immigrants from US soil—many of whom had American citizenship—and drag them back across the border. It was a move that would make Donald Trump blush, yet Attorney General Herbert Brownell okayed the law, which would be given a name far too offensive to repeat here.

Not long after this move, the government passed the *Communist Control Act of 1954,* which was signed by President Dwight Eisenhower in August. The move would strictly forbid any form of communist leanings shown by any political party in the States, and evidence of such perceived atrocities would be punishable by jail time or deportation. Head of the FBI, J. Edgar Hoover, actually spoke out against the ruling, claiming that such a decision would force any known communists underground, therefore making it harder for his people to keep an eye on them.

Tensions were running high in Britain and Ireland too, and the IRA, after years of relative inactivity, successfully raided a British military barracks in Armagh, Northern Ireland. The raid, which had been planned for a while, would go off without a hitch, thanks to an insider who had applied for and gained admittance into the British Army years before. The IRA would make off with over 400 weapons, including machine guns, rifles, and Sten submachine guns. The raid caused severe unrest among the British, and over the following few decades, the IRA's reign of terror would become the stuff of nightmares.

Conditions in Britain continued to improve, though, and '54 saw Winston Churchill turn 80. Such an achievement while still in power proved the endless love that the public held toward him and his superhuman strength. Carrying the weight of a nation on your shoulders is backbreaking and stressful for a young person, never mind a man in his eighties, so for someone to do it at this age showed a determination that is almost unimaginable. It would be another year before the great man stepped down, and his achievement has yet to be equaled in British politics.

The World Cup in '54 was held in Switzerland and would be shown on TVs around the globe for the first time. The competition, although popular, had yet to take on the sort of fervent following that it is known for today. Some memorable moments still took place, not least the crowning of a West German side that had only been allowed into the tournament for the first time following the war.

The Germans, who had lost to heavy favorites Hungary 8-3 earlier in the tournament, somehow managed to lift the title against the same team in the final. They showed the toughness and resilience that they would become renowned for in the world of football in later years, and the Miracle of Bern saw over 60,000 people cram into the Wankdorf Stadion to watch the game play out. An unfit Ferenc Puskás couldn't lift his team to the heights they had shown over the previous few years, and the West Germans ran out 3-2 winners.

After the hell of the previous decade, '54 continued to build on the improvements made in the early fifties. People were starting to make positive plans again, and the things they were trying to achieve were mindblowing. Consumerism was exploding, and finally, the public was earning enough money to treat themselves every once in a while. On rare occasions, this was even done extravagantly, with the purchase of a new color TV for the family or the latest Frank Sinatra record. It was a beautiful time that many people who had lived through the atrocities of the forties never thought they would see again.

There was some trepidation and fear, sure, but there has never been a point in time when this hasn't been the case. The difference is how we as human beings and as a community face up to it, and during the fifties, the public stood together. Of course, there would be times when they fell, but as the new sound of rock and roll began to fill the airwaves and Hollywood produced one wonder after another, there always seemed to be somebody beside them to pick them up when they did and dust them off.

1955: The Year of James Dean

Two timeless movies were released in '55, although ticket sales did not fully reflect their genius at the time. Both *East of Eden* and *Rebel Without a Cause* are considered classics today, and they were extremely well-received by critics at the time, but they came out at a period when war-time epics and Disney movies were the big box office draws. The people who *did* go were blown away by the drama and acting in *Eden* and *Rebel*, and the 24-year-old star of both, James Dean, became America's shining light almost overnight.

Dean had appeared in movies before in minor, uncredited roles, and his appearance in that Coca-Cola commercial a few years prior had given the nation a glimpse of his staggering good looks. He had even shown up in the odd episode of random television shows but never in the leading man role that he would make his own. His acting, though, was what everyone was talking about in 1955, and the director of *East of Eden*, Elia Kazan, credited Dean with something that up until then was an unknown trait of actors, and that was 'improvisation.'

While filming the John Steinbeck masterpiece, James Dean would improvise several of the now-iconic moments in the movie, namely the scene where he is being rejected by his father, played by Raymond Massey. In that scene, after handing his father money he has earned and desperately seeking the man's approval, his dad shuns him in what would have already been a heartbreaking scene. Dean was meant to run away following this but instead leaped forward and dragged Massey in for a rough embrace. Taken aback by this, and seeing James Dean crying in character, Raymond Massey's shocked face only adds to the quality of the whole thing.

Dean's second movie to come out that year, *Rebel Without a Cause*, was released in late October, almost a month after its star was tragically killed when his Porsche 550 Spyder collided with another car on US Route 466. The passenger in James Dean's car and the other driver would survive, but Dean, who had always loved fast cars and racing, was killed instantly. His death sent shockwaves around the world, and we can only imagine how brightly his star might have shone if the accident had never occurred and his career had continued to blossom.

On hearing of the actor's death, a young Elvis Presley is said to have broken down in tears in his motel room during one of his maiden tours of the South. A sentimental man by nature, the soon-to-be King, was inconsolable for hours as he mourned a man he had never physically met. Nearing the end of '55, Elvis's career was really starting to take off, but the introduction of a man named 'Colonel' Tom Parker into his life changed things considerably.

Parker, who would proclaim himself as Elvis's manager, had a way of convincing the young man that every decision he made was for his own good, while in truth, he was taking the lion's share of all the income while Elvis ran himself into the ground. His iron-clad grip on Elvis would only tighten through the years, and the colonel made sure to squeeze every dime he could out of his famous client.

Almost like a sign of what lay in Elvis's future, the first-ever McDonalds opened its doors in April of 1955. The restaurant had been around a few years before, and the two brothers who ran it, Richard and Maurice McDonald, were mildly successful with their self-service hamburger joint. When Ray Kroc approached them a year earlier, he proclaimed that there was so much more potential in the company. He convinced them to let him do all the promotional work, and he would start opening up franchises all over the US if they gave him more control. The brothers were blown away by the idea of such expansion to their little enterprise, and they agreed to sign over the rights. The deal they accepted? One-half of one percent of sales of the franchises going forward.

Keeping up with the fast-paced, fast-food, fast-life attitude sweeping the States, the first signs of soda bottles being replaced came that year. The James Vernor Company of Detroit was the first to use cans instead when they released their six-pack of ginger ale. Dr. Pepper soon followed suit, and a gimmick that had been aimed solely at the picnic market would gradually become the norm. Surprisingly, Coca-Cola lagged behind on the trend, and it would be a decade before they swallowed their pride and rode the wave of cans over glass bottles.

Britain was shaken by the resignation of Winston Churchill. The man who had returned to power years before reluctantly stepped down as Prime Minister in April of '55. He was to be replaced by his right-hand man of 15 years, Anthony Eden. The public wasn't exactly ecstatic at this appointment, but they believed that their new leader would be good if Churchill had approved him and trusted his opinion for so long. In an unprecedented act of respect, Queen Elizabeth and her husband, Prince Philip, joined the Churchills for dinner on their last night at 10 Downing Street. Such a gesture had never before been made, and it only went to prove the mammoth respect that was held for the man who had brought the nation through the most gruesome war in history.

Football saw Chelsea win the league championship for the first time, which also happened to be the first-ever major trophy of any kind in their history. Before the club was run by a Russian billionaire, they had to depend on the shrewd management of Arsenal legend

Ted Drake to lead them to victory. In a twist that would have most modern-day football fans in hysterics, Liverpool could only manage an 11th place finish, which just so happened to be in the Second Division too. It was a rough time for the club, but they would go on to great success a couple of decades later.

After losing the final of the NFL championship three years running, the Cleveland Browns lifted the title for the second year in a row in '55 when they defeated the Los Angeles Rams in front of over 85,000 people at the LA Memorial Coliseum. It would round off a fantastic five-year stint of the Browns reaching consecutive finals, a run that started in 1951. American football was changing, both in popularity and in rules, as two major changes came that year, including the now essential rule imploring that the ball is dead the second any part of the carrier's body hits the ground apart from their hands and feet.

With all of the advancements taking place the world over, there was still so much more that needed to be fixed. Something that was never more evident than on December 1, 1955, in Montgomery, Alabama. It was the day when a young African American woman by the name of Rosa Parks refused to give up her seat on a bus when the driver insisted that she do so for the white passengers. Mrs. Parks said "no," and remained sitting until the police arrived and arrested her.

Her actions would spawn the Montgomery Bus Boycott, during which all of the local African American residents refused to take any buses. As they made up the majority of bus riders, it was a big hit for the city. The standoff would last a whole year, but in the end, the U.S. Supreme Court finally ruled that segregation on local transportation was unconstitutional. The person who led the Montgomery Bus Boycott alongside Rosa was a young man named Reverend Martin Luther King Jr.

All of these types of events were stains on the history of the human race, but we must always concentrate on the heroes instead of the villains. Without the likes of Rosa Parks standing up for what is right, the atrocities would have continued. It can be hard to look past the nastiness of our past sometimes, but we must remember that things are constantly changing for the better. The fifties gave us some of the greatest thinkers, revolutionaries, musicians, movies, and technological breakthroughs imaginable. Although there was sadness and suffering, we must always learn to remember the beautiful moments, too.

We may have seen the resignation of someone who is considered the greatest leader in the history of Britain—and probably the world— in '55, but the nation he left behind was rising again. Consumerism was at its highest in decades, and across the Atlantic in the States, 70% of families now owned a car. As always, Britain was never far behind their cousins, with TVs and other extravagances becoming part of the average person's life.

In fact, Britain was starting to yearn for all things American, especially the younger people. Rock and roll, diners, fancy cars, slicked-back hair, and going to the pictures were becoming everything that British kids desired. Their parents were probably a little more trepidatious, but if history has taught us anything, it's that the youth will always find a way to get what they want, even if it takes a little time to get there.

1956: Revolution and Tea-Drinking Chimps

This was the year when Elvis Presley became a global superstar, the likes of which the world had never seen before. Everything seemed to fall into place at the very moment it needed to. TV was more accessible than ever. Almost every home had a record player. The world was looking forward again. Consumerism was on the rise, and rock and roll was ready to explode. Had anyone else stepped into the limelight at that very moment, things would indeed not have worked out the same way, but Elvis Presley seemed to have been almost designed to fill the void that nobody knew had been there until he arrived.

By the end of 1956, Presley had astonishingly produced 17 hits that managed to break into the *Billboard Top 100*, with three of them—"Love Me Tender," "Heartbreak Hotel," and "Don't Be Cruel"—all hitting the number one spot. Two albums released that same year, *Elvis Presley* and *Elvis*, spent 10 weeks and a month on the top of the *Billboard Top Albums Chart*, respectively. His debut, *Elvis Presley*, was the first rock and roll album to reach the summit of the mainstream charts, and a movement that had been seen as a passing fad by most proved that it was here to stay.

Under the misguided leadership of Colonel Tom Parker, young Elvis spent '56 being worked into the ground. Along with the recording of two albums and endless singles, the recently-crowned King of Rock and Roll churned out his first movie, *Love Me Tender*, in November and managed to squeeze in 143 live shows across 79 different cities. To top it all off, he had to then make 11 separate appearances on an array of variety shows, including his two iconic performances on the *Ed Sullivan Show*.

Before all of this, his star had only really shone over the Southern states, but by the time '56 came to a close, he was the most popular celebrity the world had ever seen. But it was also apparent that his manager was determined to hold the kid up by his ankles and shake him until every last cent fell out onto the floor.

In cinema, the golden touch of producer/director Cecil B. DeMille was on display again, as his latest epic, *The Ten Commandments*, left all others in its wake at the box office. The man who had also directed *Cleopatra* and *The Greatest Show on Earth* would never direct another movie again after *The Ten Commandments* wrapped. Still, he ended his career on his own terms, it seemed, as this is generally considered his greatest work. He would pass away in 1959, but the man known as the pioneer of all films left behind a legacy that can never be equaled in the world of movies.

The Suez Crisis in '56 threatened to disrupt the rise in economic fortunes that had been growing in the Western World in recent years. After a couple of years of tension, Egyptian President Gamal Abdel Nasser nationalized the canal that was originally built under the supervision of French diplomat Ferdinand de Lesseps in the 1800s. The Suez Canal had been used mainly for the transportation of petroleum to most of Europe, and without it, Britain and France stood to lose two-thirds of the oil they used each year.

The British-French-Israeli alliance that tried to fight against the decision was met with resistance from the Soviets as well as Egypt. With some interference from the States following this, the Cold War, which had been simmering for so long, threatened to boil over. The Egyptians stood their ground, though, and by the end of the year, Britain, France, and Israel withdrew all of their troops. It was another reminder that the outbreak of war was always just one wrong step away.

Almost unbelievably, the use of heroin as a recreational drug was only outlawed in Britain in June of '56. A law like this had been passed in the United States 30 years before, as they had seen a staggering rise in heroin dependency and addiction, but in the UK, it hadn't really been viewed as a problem up until then. Much of this can be attributed to a lack of education on the subject, but it can also be viewed in the sense that it was just seen as one of many lesser problems to be dealt with at the time. Now that rebuilding after the war was mostly done, other issues which had been pushed aside for later could suddenly be looked at.

Jazz drummer Dizzy Reece, who had moved to London in 1948 at the age of 17, spoke of the heroin issue in London at the time. He claimed that, yes, some people in the nightclub scene back then were taking heroin, but only a very small amount, and usually in the privacy of their own home. He went on to say that because the drug was sold over the counter, people really didn't know the full dangers of it. Reece was quoted as saying, "I do remember people queuing up outside Boots chemist at midnight to get their heroin pills on prescription" (BBC News, 2006).

With the trend of rock and roll growing, a coffee bar on Old Compton Street, London, was bought by a couple of Australian wrestlers named Paul "Dr. Death" Lincoln and Ray "rebel" Hunter, who turned it into a hip music venue in early 1956. They kept the original name, 2i's, and pretty soon, the place became a haven for young rock bands to come and rip it up on the small stage at the back. The list of musicians who started out at 2i's is far too broad to put here, but some of the most popular would be Cliff Richard, The Vipers, Hank Marvin, and Adam Faith. Several more venues such as 2i's began to sprout up as the rock movement began to truly take hold in Britain.

TV was really taking off in the UK too, and the television company Granada Television (now known as ITV) first aired in 1956. The station, which mainly covered the Northwest of England, would soon become a staple of British life. Through the years, it became known for such programs as *Coronation Street*, *Sherlock Holmes*, *The Krypton Factor*, *The Royal Family*, and *University Challenge*. It is still one of the UK's most-watched channels today.

Something that explained the sheer growth of television in Britain in the fifties was the rise in profits following the debut of the much-loved PG Tips ad campaign in '56, which showed several chimps in human clothing sitting around a kitchen table and drinking tea. The voice-overs used to show what the chimps were supposedly saying was a new concept, and it became a craze soon after, both in television and in comedic movies.

Advertising on television had become huge, and the slots between TV shows were replacing that of radio. PG Tips had been the fourth-highest selling tea bag in Britain before the first airing of the chimp advert, but they were number one within two years. Another aspect that shows the influence of television in Britain—and around the world—was when PG Tips dropped the chimp-based adverts in the sixties, only to see sales fall drastically. They brought them back in the seventies and climbed to the top once more.

In Northern Ireland, the re-emergence of a more brutal Irish Republican Army (IRA) resulted in the terrorist group starting what would be a six-year border campaign. It would involve guerilla tactics, primarily aimed at British military bases and personnel, and was a continuation of the raid on a barracks in Armagh two years before. Although the campaign was a military failure, in the end, many IRA members and sympathizers saw it as a moral victory, as it kept their name alive and drew in the next generation of soldiers.

A violent revolution was in the air in Cuba too, when a young law student named Fidel Castro landed back in Havana amidst social unrest and burgeoning civil war. Castro and 160 of his rebels had launched an unsuccessful attack on an army barracks in Santiago two years prior, and the failed attempt had led to his imprisonment, along with his brother Raul. They were given amnesty in early 1955 and released, and Castro and his brother fled to Mexico.

On his return in December of '56, Castro and 81 of his men were attacked by Batista's army as soon as they landed. Most were killed, but the few who escaped included Fidel, his brother, and Ernesto "Che" Guevara. The 12 men regrouped in the mountains of Sierra Maestra and soon began a series of guerilla attacks against Batista and his forces. The rebellion would rage for several years yet, and many cases of arrests, torture, and execution would take place before things began to settle down somewhat.

It really was a time for the youth in 1956, as the older generation started to see what young people could achieve for the first time in decades. Without the two previous wars to take away the majority of young adults, the fifties' kids were thriving, which was shown by the creation of the Duke of Edinburgh Awards (DofE) in '56. Prince Philip had started the organization in an attempt to encourage those between the ages of 15-18 to strive for self-improvement and teamwork. This wonderful idea soon spread, and today, over 144 nations worldwide now hold the ceremony each year.

Youth again was coming out on top, this time in football, as Sir Matt Busby's Busby Babes lifted the league title for only the fourth time in Manchester United's history. It was gratifying for a manager who had rebuilt his team on a system of bringing the kids through the ranks and molding them into world-beaters. Although so much of this would be undone in a couple of years, by 1956, the Red Devils' brand of football and philosophy was unique.

Someone who was not considered young by any means was still going against the grain in '56, as footballing legend Stanley Mathews just finished ahead of another genius, Ferenc Puskas, to the European Footballer of the Year Award. Although an amazing achievement in its own right, we must always remember that Sir Stanley did it at the ripe old age of 41. For a man who would go on to play at the top level until he was 50, this might have seemed normal, but Matthews had always seemed to be a different breed from the rest of us.

There seemed to be revolution in the air the world over in '56. Although some of it was unsavory, for the most part, it was just the younger generation finding their way out of the rubble through music, television, sports, and expression. These kinds of movements are rare in history, and the spirit of the fifties should be put on the same level as the French Renaissance of the 15th century. Although this may seem a little over the top, it really isn't when you consider everything that the fifties generation created and what they left for those that followed to build on.

They may not have all made their miracles on a canvas, like the artists of the Renaissance, but their work is no less impressive. Such creations as the color television, Walt Disney animation, Ralph Elison's *Invisible Man*, and Elvis Presley's debut album are all masterpieces in their own right. We must never forget that the people of the fifties achieved all of this amid racial tensions, the Cold War, oppression, economic struggle, and rebuilding after the Second World War. When we take these terrible hindrances into account, and so many others, the wonders of a decade that gave us so much good can maybe be seen in the perspective it deserves.

1957: Babies Boom

The world was expanding and improving at a rapid rate by 1957, and this particular period is regarded as the peak of the Baby Boomer years. In '57, an average of 4.3 million babies were born in the United States alone, with the previous two years hitting the 4 million mark too. Put this against the total in 1945—2.8 million—and we can begin to see the massive difference in how the world was growing.

Families were getting larger once again, and for the first time that century, parents didn't fear that their children would go hungry or be dragged off to war by the time they turned 18. Enthusiasm was the order of the day, and this is something that would be heavily reflected in the sixties. But the fifties were sowing the seeds, and the kids who were being raised would be the young adults who made so many changes through the end of the decade and into the next.

Although it wouldn't be termed the "Space Race" for another few years, the Soviets made the first move in space exploration when they successfully launched the satellite Sputnik 1 into orbit. America and the Soviets were in the midst of the Cold War, and anything that either country could do to show the other one up was considered a victory. This move by the Soviets was a big win for them, and they would lead the Space Race throughout the following decade, right up until the end.

The conflict in Vietnam took another turn when an anti-communist campaign in South Vietnam was formed in an attempt to decimate suspected communist members. The Chinese had begun leaning toward communism in 1949, and this influence had spread into Vietnam. Almost 2,000 communist members and sympathizers were killed, and over 65,000 more arrested. America had already supplied the anti-communists with weapons and equipment, but it would be a long time before the US would send troops over themselves and become directly involved in the war.

In a moment in time that would mirror events in 2020, the Asian flu pandemic ripped through the world in '57. It would go on to kill what is suspected to be between 2-4 million people before it was contained a year later. The deadly flu first showed up in Southern China around March, but it was not reported globally. The Chinese wouldn't become a member of the World Health Organization (WHO) until 1981, and their government did not feel the need to inform anyone else about the cases they had witnessed or the severity of the disease in '57.

Although the Suez Crisis came to an abrupt end early in '57, the backlash was too severe for Sir Anthony Eden to come back from. The man who had stepped in after the resignation of Winston Churchill saw his short tenure as Prime Minister come to an end in January when Harold Macmillan replaced him. Macmillan was elected leader of the Conservative Party two weeks later, and he immediately set about restoring UK-US relations, which had been severely damaged during the Suez Crisis.

Another hectic year for Elvis saw him switch his attention to Hollywood, as Colonel Parker signed him up for two more movies, *Loving You* and *Jailhouse Rock*. The King had always dreamed of being seen as a serious actor, but the Colonel believed there was more money in schmaltzy movies in which Elvis could sing. With these types of films, they could release an accompanying soundtrack, and even more cash could be drained out of the Elvis brand.

Elvis would see his bank balance reach heights that he could have never dreamed, and in the spring of '57, he purchased his new home, Graceland. He would move his parents in too, and as the whirlwind of fame and fortune continued to whip up around the 22-year-old. But he was brought back down to Earth with a bang in December when, as he prepared to celebrate Christmas with his family, Elvis received notice of being drafted by the U.S. Army.

In football, the mercurial John Charles finished the season with 38 goals, even though his club Leeds United could only manage an eighth-place finish, which only goes to show how far ahead of the rest of his teammates he was. This staggering achievement alerted the world's biggest clubs, and Italian giants Juventus won the race to sign the Welshman for £65,000 that summer, a British transfer record at the time.

Charles, who could play at both center-back or up front, was a massive success in Italy. He was the top scorer and player of the year in his first season, scoring 28 goals and guiding his new team to the league championship. The partnership he formed with Enrique Omar Sivori and Giampiero Boniperti became known as The Holy Trident, and they are still loved today. His 108 goals in 155 games saw him win three league titles and two domestic cups in his five-year stint for the Italians. John Charles was voted the greatest foreigner ever to play for Juventus in 1997 by their fans, beating the likes of Michel Platini and Liam Brady for the honor.

The league title in England was retained by an ever-improving Manchester United side, as they finished eight points ahead of second-placed Spurs. Tom Finney's wizardry that season could only help Preston North End to a third-place finish, where they finished one spot above the 42-year-old Stanley Matthews-driven Blackpool. The fifties were clearly shaping up as a decade for the younger generation, though, as was proven by the Busby Babes claiming the top spot once again.

Like the 2i's coffee bar in London and the other rock music venues springing up around Britain in the fifties, possibly the most important one of all time opened its doors for the first time in January of 1957. It wouldn't happen in some trendy city like Paris, New York, or London, but in Liverpool. The Cavern Club would be the place where four mop-topped rockers would first ply their trade in a few years, and it is synonymous with the blossoming rock scene of the fifties and sixties.

Unbeknownst to anyone, another first was taking place in Liverpool in '57, when a young kid named John Lennon first shook the hand of another scruffy teenager by the name of Paul McCartney. A rag-tag skiffle group, led by Lennon, was performing a lunchtime set at a garden fete in Woolton, Liverpool, when Paul popped along to watch on a whim. Surrounded by cake stalls, craft tables, and smiling families, the most important partnership in music crossed paths, and the first step in the creation of the Beatles was taken.

Something else far less pleasant began that year in Liverpool, too, when the largest abattoir in the North of England was forced to shut down because of foot and mouth disease. Several cases of the deadly disease were found when the premises were inspected, and a lot of people's jobs were put on hold as the nation held its breath. It would spread, though, and over the next year, foot and mouth would affect over 20 different counties and result in the slaughter of more than 30,000 animals.

The Toddlers Truce was finally abolished in 1957. The policy was an agreement made by television companies across Britain after the war pertaining that they would cease all broadcasting between 6 and 7 p.m. to allow parents to put their kids to bed. Before the age of TiVo and Sky Plus, the people who watched their TV had to do so live. If there was a program they wished to view, they would have to watch it at the exact time it aired. If they didn't, then they would most probably never get the chance.

The Baby Boomers were in full swing by 1957. The decade of peace and love was yet to come, but the parents of the fifties appeared to be getting the hint and enjoying themselves in the process. Times continued to look up, and this was shown in the way the public was opening their minds to new things. It seemed that a stuffiness was being aired out of the world, and unique views and ideas were popping up at every moment.

Humankind had sent an object into orbit, and the career of one Elvis Presley seemed to be doing the exact same thing. The sky was not the limit anymore, and people were dreaming bigger than they ever had. Anything was possible, and the generation of the fifties was going to make sure they did everything they could to achieve them.

1958: Microchips and M1

The Great Chinese Famine began in 1958 and would last for almost a decade. Chairman Mao, whose Communist Party had come into power in '49, had tried to put his new plan into action, but the *Great Leap Forward* was an absolute disaster. Millions of farmers saw their crops taken by government officials as they tried to put a structure into place that couldn't possibly have worked. The first three years of the famine were horrendous, and it is widely regarded as the deadliest one in the history of humankind.

Reports on the total death toll vary, and they will never be fully understood, but with numbers mentioned between 20-50 million, we know that it was one of the most horrific man-made errors of all time. Stories of cannibalism, bodies piled up in every village, and severe oppression by the authorities will always leave a bad taste in the mouths of the Chinese people. So the fact that they managed to rebuild so impressively in the years that followed speaks volumes for their character.

October of '58 saw the first commercial transatlantic flights become available to the public. BOAC started their service on the 4th, and flights between London and New York opened up to public amazement. Such feats were still astonishing, and before then, this type of journey would have taken a very long time. Pan Am followed suit by the end of the month when they announced a New York to Paris service that would be achieved using the *Boeing 707*.

These advancements in flight would come a little too late for the Manchester United team when their plane crashed after takeoff in West Germany on February 6, 1958. Of the 44 passengers on board, 23 would die. The tragedy which took away so much of the United team— and several supporters and staff—would be forever remembered as one of the darkest days in the history of sports.

Following their recent domination of the domestic league, the Busby Babes had set their sights on the European Cup. Just before they boarded the plane in Munich, the team had just overcome Red Star Belgrade to reach the semi-finals, and they were many people's picks to go all the way.

Among the players that passed away was young Duncan Edwards, who would fight for his life for another 15 days before finally succumbing to his injuries. Edwards was regarded by most of the people who worked with him at the time to be the greatest player they had ever seen. Having become the youngest footballer to play in the top flight three years earlier, he would do the same for the national side not long after. His physical strength and authoritative nature made him a fan favorite, and when he died at the age of 21, he had amassed a staggering 177 appearances for his club already. He was one of eight players who perished in the Munich Air Disaster.

Eight years after a 9-year-old Pele told his father he would win him the World Cup, the young man delivered on his promise. The competition in Sweden, held in a Scandinavian country for the first time, was a roaring success. The flair and passion shown by the Brazilian team were being beamed across the globe, and the 17-year-old wonderkid would go on to score two more goals in the final. His first, against the hosts, has been replayed millions of times, as he chipped the ball over the head of a Swedish defender before volleying it into the bottom corner.

Stateside saw the NFL final be decided by a sudden-death overtime, something which had never happened before. On a cold day in December, the Baltimore Colts and New York Giants lit up Yankee Stadium in what has since been deemed The Greatest Game Ever Played. It would finish 23-17 in favor of the Colts, and in a nationwide poll carried out by sports journalists in 2019, it was voted the greatest game in the sport's 100-year history.

Britain continued to expand, and construction on the M1 motorway began before the end of the year. It was to be the first-ever inter-urban motorway to be made in the UK, and it marked a time of great prosperity and foresight. At 193 miles, it would make travel between Yorkshire—and its surrounding areas—to London a whole lot easier and quicker, of course. Britain was truly on the rise.

Another leap forward came in the scientific world that year, when Texas Instruments engineer Jack Kilby invented the microchip. The first demonstration of what the chip could do was not held for another two years, and even then, its intricacies seemed to scare and confuse buyers. There were no genuine bids for the invention, as people thought that there would just be no use for it. Of course, it would catch on, and without it, we would not have laptops, cell phones, Xbox, and basically every other technological marvel we take for granted today.

After his draft number had come up in December of the previous year, young Elvis Presley had been given an extra few months back in the States to finish filming his latest movie, *King Creole*. By March, though, the American government had waited long enough, and Elvis was officially inducted into the United States Army. His slimy manager Tom Parker was on the ball as always, and he made sure to have a photographer at the ready as the King signed his papers. Whatever he could do to milk the situation, he would.

Elvis, for his part, seemed calm and collected, with no signs of petulance or arrogance suggesting that he was too important to become a lowly grunt. Shipped off to Germany, the young man from Memphis was apart from his mother for the first time in his life. He had traveled around America before, sure, but Gladys had only ever been a car trip away. For a loyal family man like Elvis, this would be the hardest part of the whole ordeal.

Rock and roll had fully taken hold in Britain too, and among all of the records in the genre clogging the shelves in the music stores across the country, the UK was now producing their own rockstars. A young Cliff Richard became the first person to reach number one in the British charts with a rock and roll number. "Move It" was written, produced, and recorded in England and is known as the first-ever wholly British rock song to top the *UK Singles Chart*.

Another first in British entertainment came in the form of comedy when the long-running movie series *Carry On* released *Carry On Sergeant*. It would go on to surpass its budget 10 times over, and the roaring success of the film made instant stars of its cast. Kenneth Williams, Hattie Jacques, Kenneth Connor, Terry Scott, and Charles Hawtry would make many more of the much-loved movies together. The over-the-top raunchy comedy was a hit, and the series would become a massive part of British pop culture through the years. Amazingly, there have been 31 *Carry On* films produced to date, with many more Christmas specials, TV episodes, and stage plays.

In America, cinema had gone in another direction too. After the demand for war epics and big-budget blockbusters, it seemed that the comedy craze was not just restricted to Britain. *Uncle Mame, No Time for Sergeants*, and *Gigi* all finished in the top five at the box office in '58, with the number one spot being taken by *South Pacific*, a romantic musical. Drama and war flicks were still being made, but it seemed that in 1958, the people going to the cinema wanted something a little less stressful for the time being.

In a year that saw the construction of the first major motorway in Britain—and the implementation of parking meters too—it is clear to see that the UK was a nation on the rise. The Western World was progressing as a whole, but it seemed that some parts of Asia were beginning to struggle, as can be seen by the Great Famine in China. Still, the continent would manage to get out of it over time, proving that the human spirit is an unbelievable thing.

For football fans, the year will only be remembered for two things, namely the Munich Air Disaster and the maiden appearance on TV screens of a young Pele. Both will always bring contrasting emotions, but the important thing is never to forget. Things moved forward, and with the tragic events in Munich driving on the surviving members of the Manchester United team, they soon rebuilt and created many more fantastic memories.

Resourcefulness like this is what makes the world what it is, and overcoming adversity is something that can always be associated with the fifties generation. It was all about making hay when the sun shines, and if it didn't, then they just found another way. It is hard to contemplate something as mind-blowing as the microchip being invented so long ago, but this creation is a testament to the mentality of those that came before.

1959: NASA Joins the Space Race

After years of unrest, Fulgencio Batista was finally overthrown on July 26, when Fidel Castro and his army took control of Cuba. The new leader instantly went about assuming military and political power. The Americans saw Castro as a threat, and their future assassination attempts and moves to overthrow him would lead to the Cuban president leaning toward the ideals of the Soviets and the military support they could offer.

Asia continued to struggle, and the Dalai Lama was forced to flee Tibet as the Chinese communist views became more intense, and their anti-religious legislation took hold. There had been many protests and organized rallies in Tibet concerning Chinese oppression, but they had never been anything more than scattered. In March of '59, they exploded, and a nationwide revolt broke out. This sudden burst of violence prompted the Dali Lama to escape the country, as Chinese forces crushed anyone who dared to rise up against them.

The American Toy Fair in New York City saw the debut of what would soon become the world's most famous doll. Barbie, who stood at 11 inches in height and with long, flowing blonde locks, represented the look that Hollywood had decided all women should have. It was the first mass-produced doll in American history to be made with adult features, and the woman who created it, Ruth Handler, would use the money she made from co-founding toy manufacturers Mattel to promote her latest creation.

Amazingly, the Barbie doll was first marketed as a gag gift for adult men, and it was to be sold over the counter at bars and tobacco stores. But the adult-themed doll caught on fast with the young girls, and through a coexisting deal that Mattel had with Disney, they were able to advertise Barbie at the perfect times to all of the children who desired it. Named after Handler's daughter, Barbara, she would soon release the doll's male equivalent, this time named after her son, Ken.

With the sixties fast approaching, NASA announced via a press conference that they had named their first-ever official astronauts. The USSR had already taken the first moral victory in the burgeoning Space Race when they successfully sent Sputnik 1 into orbit. Now that the

Americans were lagging behind, they hoped that their announcement of the seven ex-military test pilots would show that they meant business. NASA went on to declare that they would have crewed orbital flights in progress by 1961. It was a bold statement, and it was just a taste of the back-and-forth that would escalate between the Soviets and the States in the coming years.

With the Cold War still in full effect, the Soviets made a move that angered the Americans when they allowed British Prime Minister Harold Macmillan to spend 10 days visiting Moscow. The trip was far from a sightseeing expedition, and Macmillan was really there to hold talks with the Soviet leader, Nikita Khrushchev. It was the first time a British politician had done such a thing since Winston Churchill during the Second World War, and it is still seen as a massive step in the repairing process of Anglo/Soviet relations.

The meteoric rise of rock and roll took a devastating hit in February of 1959 when a small plane carrying rock pioneer Buddy Holly and some of his bandmates crashed in a frozen cornfield in Iowa. All four people on board were killed instantly, including the 21-year-old pilot and up-and-coming music stars Richie Valens and J.P. Richardson. With such a loss of talent going down in one plane, Don McLean would be inspired to write the song "American Pie" in 1971, with the timeless lyric referring to "the day the music died."

With Elvis now stationed in Germany—and meeting a 14-year-old girl named Pricilla—the death of Buddy Holly seemed even more devastating to rock. Luckily for the genre, the likes of Presley and Holly had done enough in the preceding years to make sure that the movement was too far along to go away any time soon. Rock and roll had become too important to the kids, and an array of soon-to-be legends that had been influenced by those that came before were picking up guitars in their bedrooms the world over as they prepared to blow the doors off the sixties.

The TV show *Juke Box Jury* arrived in June of '59. The show featured musicians and showbiz stars of the time who came onto the BBC show to judge the potential of the latest records. Some of the guest judges to appear over the years included Cilla Black, Spike Milligan, Roy Orbison, Johnny Mathis, and Alfred Hitchcock. It became so popular that by October of the same year it debuted, it was pulling in weekly viewing figures of over nine million. *Juke Box Jury* continued to grow in popularity, and by 1963 it was so hot that they even secured appearances by all four of the Beatles.

One of the most miraculous events in football happened a year after one of the most devastating, and it involved the same team. Manchester United had lost eight players in the Munich Air Disaster, yet they somehow managed to challenge for the domestic league the very next season. They would fall just short, but their second-place finish after such a setback only strengthened the legend that was forming around Sir Matt Busby.

The league crown went to Wolverhampton Wanderers in the end, as they claimed a third title in their proud history. The 1958/59 season was also the first year that the English league saw the addition of the Fourth Division. But the year would truly belong to the players and fans of the Red Devils, as they seemed to single-handedly epitomize everything that the fifties stood for: Resilience, strength, and endurance.

After The Greatest Game Ever Played the previous year, fans were licking their lips at the prospect of another classic when the same two sides met in the NFL final once more. The Colts would be victorious again, but the 31-16 scoreline was far too one-sided for the game to be even near as memorable. The action took place at the Memorial Stadium and remains the only NFL final to be played in Baltimore to date.

Shot on the biggest budget allocated to a movie before '59, the William Wyler-directed *Ben Hur* was seen as somewhat of a gamble by movie execs, given the amount of money spent on production. Comedies and musicals had made a comeback the previous year, and such swashbuckling epics seemed to be on the way out. But *Ben Hur* was such a masterpiece that even the most cynical of movie-goers were lured into the theaters to see what all the fuss was about.

Charlton Heston, who was fond of starring in blockbusters, was the perfect leading man for a movie of such magnitude. His star power had been seen in *The Ten Commandments* and *The Greatest Show on Earth*, to name a few, so even having his name attached meant some guaranteed success even before a camera rolled. It brought in $149 million on a $15 million budget, cementing Heston as the go-to actor when in need of a leading man.

Another movie that surpassed its budget many times over in '59 was *Some Like It Hot*. In one of Marilyn Monroe's last appearances on film, she gave a performance that would forever leave her mark on the movie business. The lady who changed the acting world for women through her perseverance and passion was lauded for her acting in *Some Like It Hot*, and most critics consider it not only to be her greatest role but one of the best movies ever made.

Computers and technology were starting to become more and more prevalent in everyday life. The microchip had been invented the year before, and in August of 1959, Barclays became the first bank in Britain to install a computer in the hopes of making a gradual switch to digital bookkeeping. It was a bold move by the banking chain, as the single machine set them back a staggering £125,000. It would prove to be wise foresight, though, and in time, the need to handwrite every transaction would be a thing of the past.

As America continued their need to have everything bigger and better, they went one step further when they embraced Alaska and Hawaii as new states. With these two additions to the nation, they were up to a nice round 50, with Hawaii having been voted in by its residents in a massive 93% landslide. It was yet another sign of the coming together of the world that was trying to occur, although there would be many bumps in the road along the way.

*****

As the fifties came to a close, it seemed that a real sense of purpose had settled in the world. Of course, conflicts were still happening in parts, but unfortunately, this is true of any period in history. All the people knew was that it had been a decade of relative peace following the devastation of the two wars that took up the first half of the century.

It wasn't a decade that was as free as the sixties or as groovy as the seventies, but neither of those wonderful periods in time could have occurred if they hadn't stood on the shoulders of giants. Everything good about the following years in our existence comes from those who came before, and if there was ever a decade to follow, then the fifties surely was it.

A line in the sand had been drawn as 1950 began, and even though most people lived in fear of more war breaking out, they strived to move forward throughout the decade. So many astonishing changes can be attributed to this great decade in an array of areas ranging from music to space travel. Where would the former be without Elvis, and how would the latter have been achieved without Sputnik 1 being launched by the Soviets? All of these things and so many more only became real because of the fifties generation, and as we live our lives today, we must always do so with complete and utter admiration for those who came before.

References

Branigan, T. (2017, November 25). *China's Great Famine: the true story*. The Guardian; The Guardian. www.theguardian.com/world/2013/jan/01/china-great-famine-book-tombstone

Duffy, J. (2006, January 25). When heroin was legal. *News.bbc.co.uk*. http://news.bbc.co.uk/2/hi/uk_news/magazine/4647018.stm

NPR. (2020). *NPR Choice page*. Npr.org. https://www.npr.org/2012/02/14/146862081/the-history-of-the-fbis-secret-enemies-list

Simon & Schuster. (2007). *Pele: The Autobiography*. SimonSchuster. www.simonandschuster.com/books/Pele-The-Autobiography/Pele/9781416511212

Images: All images sourced from Unsplash.com

Printed in Great Britain
by Amazon